UNDERCURRENTS Series Editor J.J. Lee

Crime and Crisis in Ireland: Justice by Illusion?

CAROLINE FENNELL

CORK UNIVERSITY PRESS

First published in 1993 by
Cork University Press
University College
Cork
Ireland

British Library Cataloguing in Publication Data

A CIP catalogue record for this book is available from the British Library

ISBN 0 902561 90 1

Typeset in Ireland by Seton Music Graphics Ltd, Co. Cork
Printed in Ireland by ColourBooks, Baldoyle, Co. Dublin

CONTENTS

Acknowledgements

Thanks to Joe Lee for inviting me to write this pamphlet and to the staff of Cork University Press for encouragement and advice in completing that task.

Although the ideas and faults are the author's own, they are the result of much stimulating discussion with colleagues and friends at UCC, and in particular with students of the UCC Law Faculty throughout the past years.

In addition, having spent 1993 abroad on sabbatical leave, I am grateful for the insights and friendship of faculty and friends at the University of West Florida, Loyola Law School, Los Angeles and Oxford. Finally much thanks and love to my parents Helen and Thomas for toleration and support.

Caroline Fennell
October 1993

1. INTRODUCTION

Criminal justice is today the stuff of common parlance. Long the preserve of an elite ruling class and its members who comprised the legal profession, it has entered the common domain. Not only does every wag in a public house have a view on the latest criminal verdict or sentence, but talk-show hosts, journalists and 'popular culture' generally are awash with tales of 'crime and punishment'. In both fact and fiction, we are daily imbued with a diet of legal happenings of the criminal variety. Each of us readily assumes the role of judge, jury and appellate court, and has a passing familiarity with legalese. To what degree is this familiarity indicative of a considered view on that part of the body politic which is our criminal justice system? When we consider tales of crime do we think of justice? If we focus on the end 'result' – level of criminal activity, number of convictions, frequency of guilty verdicts, severity of sentence – is that at the expense of what secures that end, the criminal *process*? Perceiving ourselves as crime victims may further assumptions that the crime happened as alleged, and discount the value of such obstacles to conviction. Contrast that with the view from the other perspective – that of the accused.

Recent events in Irish public and political life indicate a readiness to view criminal justice solely from a particular perspective, and a failure to question the implications of that stance. Discussion of the nature of the current system, the basis for change, the principles guiding adjustment is nonexistent. Assumptions abound as to the need for change, the effective resolution of crisis by legislation, and omnipresent is the conviction that the overall structure remains secure and cognizant of liberal values (individual rights). This pamphlet challenges those and other assumptions characterizing our current discourse on crime. It laments the poverty of public discussion and debate, and the shortsightedness of the political and legislative response; in view of the current consensus informing the 'popular view' on reform of the criminal justice system, it unapologetically takes another stance.

The role of the media in forming and feeding the tyranny of that 'popular view' is identified as crucial: facilitating political invocation of short-term responses, and public acceptance thereof. As a substitute for considered debate we have a public arena saturated with 'sound bite' criminal discourse and piecemeal legislative change. What is forgotten is the broader picture: what it is we do through the medium of the criminal justice system, and why we have fashioned it as it is. The focus here is not on the *particular* crime, the *particular* accused, the *particular* victim, but rather that those particular events form a whole, and should evolve from a considered view of what it is we try *generally* to achieve through the medium of our criminal justice system.

That our politicians have abdicated responsibility for that task in favour of legislating their way out of political crises is self-evident. Take a recent interview given by the current Minister for Justice, Ms. Maire Geoghegan-Quinn, to the *Irish Times*. Responding to a query as to whether it was time to examine what our society wants from a criminal justice system – a suggestion mooted by the Association of Garda Sergeants and Inspectors – she stated:

> As you know (the Lord Mayor of Dublin) Gay Mitchell has set up the Dublin Crime Commission. I am not a great supporter of these bureaucracies or fancy titles. I think we have a lot of reports out there, a lot of information. What we need now is action. That is why I think the Corporate Plan (the Garda Siochana Corporate Strategy Document 1993–1997) is very important; looking at our system, how we do our business and how the gardai in particular organize themselves. That would be my priority – that there should be action. That is not to say that I would not wish the Dublin Crime Commission the best of luck.[1]

What is challenged most of all by this pamphlet is precisely the view that action is a priority. By contrast it is suggested that ill-considered reaction in this context may not so much fail to be part of the solution to what ails our criminal justice system, but itself pose part of the problem.

2. PROCESS VERSUS SUBSTANCE AND THE IRISH CRIMINAL JUSTICE SYSTEM

> In both political and scientific development the sense of malfunction that can lead to crisis is prerequisite to revolution.[2]

Criminal law is as old as human nature. For as long as humans have deviated from what is deemed acceptable conduct by those around them, they have been judged and punished. From summary execution at the hands of another, to mob lynching, and the modern equivalent of 'street justice' meted out by the police, people have been deprived of life, liberty and property by their peers. The manner in which these deprivations have been executed, has been variously approved by the communities in which they occur. Indeed such approval has become the signifier of what constitutes legitimate coercion as opposed to brute force, and as the notion has developed that there are ways of dealing with such matters – the manner of response – the procedure or process has become *part of* rather than distinct from, or opposite to, the substance of the right or wrong.

So it it that limitations have been placed not just on what individual citizens can do, but on what the state can do to violators of the community's norms. That a distinction has recently re-emerged between substance and procedure in Irish criminal law, coupled with a corresponding relegation of procedure to a place of relative unimportance, is not only significant, but potentially worrisome. We are facing a situation in Ireland where once again the *substance* is all that matters: the focus is placed on the violation. Yet it may well be queried how that can be — why are limitations placed only on the citizen, not the state? There are no summary executions carried out, and if you consider Gibraltar or indeed LA,[3] look at the public response. *How* we deal with our violators has always been the hallmark of liberal societies. Nothing has changed. Justice is still executed in the courtrooms, not on the streets. Yet as William O. Douglas once remarked, governments by taking short cuts may well (in ways not so flagrant as a lynching) rewrite the history of liberty.[4] Whether such is happening in the context of the Irish criminal justice system is the focus of this pamphlet.

Criminal law and procedure in Ireland, is rooted in the 'common law'. That means it is largely unwritten, found in case-law (individual decisions) and the hearts of judges. Typically it is an older field of law, where eighteenth- or nineteenth-century cases and statutes may govern what is acceptable or unacceptable conduct (for instance the Larceny Act, 1916, still governing offences against property, and the Offences Against the Person Act, 1861, regarding non-fatal offences). That this 'calendar of crimes' may change as society and its mores change is self-evident;[5] what may be forgotten is that those changes take place within the context of the same process of adjudication as their precursors. So it is that the manner of adjudicating guilt or innocence of crimes, has itself become characteristic of the structure and readily identifiable (and visible) whatever those crimes may be. People are in large measure familiar with the process of trial, courts, jury, rules of procedure and lawyers, though they may not be overly familiar with either the detail of the criminal law, or the detail of that procedure.

How people are adjudged innocent or guilty of crimes is not just an aged question, it is also a difficult one. It poses a particular challenge to any society which values those 'rights' a citizen may thereby lose: life, liberty *or* property, and is concerned about the manner of their loss. The challenge is heightened by the difficulty of basing such an important decision on the fragility and limitations of human judgement. Hence we have built a structure which attempts to minimize the import of those fragilities and so maximize the acceptability of the result. Since the bloody and repressive regimes of the eighteenth century, that structure has changed only marginally, perhaps because we haven't got any better at making hard decisions.

Recently in Ireland however, specific procedures and provisions have started to emerge to change the 'detail' of that process. They have been aimed, in the main, at certain kinds of offences, particularly those perpetrated against women and children. They have occurred in the context of much public debate about the nature of violations and their nomination, together with concern that what is labelled unacceptable by our society, does not neglect to reflect the experiences and feelings of some of its less vocal or disenfranchised sectors.

It is also important to recall the even bigger picture – not that solely of offences against women and children, or those of a 'sexual' nature, but of criminal offences generally and how we translate allegations into crimes. The birth of a distinction between substance and procedure (at least in some areas) in Irish legislative life merits debate, yet to date has engendered little political controversy or response.

The resonances of the assumption that 'justice' and 'procedure' are somehow in conflict, and that a focus on process is somehow the antithesis of a 'fair' result, has characterized much of the recent commentary. This pamphlet challenges that assumption; asserting the very real nature of the substance/process correlation, alleging the spuriousness of those who would claim them to be distinct. The argument is largely that of Dahl's advocate who defends the democratic process on the grounds that it is strongly substantive as well as procedural, the analogy to a 'fair trial' making the argument complete:

> It is a mistake to think that procedures are somehow devoid of moral significance. I hear people say, for example, that 'procedures should not be permitted to stand in the way of justice'. Yet justice is procedural as well as substantive. Often, as in criminal trials, no process can guarantee that the outcome will be substantively just: a fair trial may still lead to a mistaken verdict. Nonetheless, it is possible to conclude that one process is more likely than another to arrive at the right result. Thus we may decide that in criminal cases a jury of one's peers is superior to any feasible alternative. At most, however, even the best designed judicial system can guarantee only procedural justice; it cannot guarantee substantive justice. A constitution can ensure a right to a fair trial; it can't absolutely guarantee that a fair trial will always lead to the right verdict. But it is precisely because no such guarantee is possible that we place such a high value on a fair trial.[6]

CRISIS AND DUALITY

Naming things is a function of how we see the world around us: it is also the manner in which we construct that reality. Criminal law names what is considered deviant in our society, but also influences what we consider to be appropriate behaviour. The 'naming' of prostitution, for example, does more than simply tell us what is forbidden or inappropriate in a society; it also defines what that inappropriateness is – how it manifests itself. That in turn informs a paradigm of gender relations and appropriate behaviour.

In this manner we as citizens internalize the social categories of crime and deviance in our society, in a manner which is supportive of the state's view as to dissent and tolerance. Summer puts it rather colourfully:

> Nuts, sluts, perverts, prostitutes, slags, murderers, psychopaths, militants, muggers, rioters, squatters and scroungers are all social censures with the potential to mobilize the forces of law, order and moral purity against targeted sections of the population.[7]

It is this phenomenon which makes it difficult to speak in any real sense of a dialogue between citizens and the state as to the substance or form of the criminal justice system. In one sense the consultation has already taken place: by the time we come to respond or react to issues in the criminal justice system, the parameters within which we will do so have already been drawn.

Particularly in a criminal justice system, where so many of the interests are central to the state's social and political structure (offences against property, wealth etc.) or indeed whet the appetite of the media by their sensationalist character; it is difficult to conceive of a 'public opinion' not circumscribed, *or* underwhelmed in its response. Public opinion and the criminal law are inextricably linked. Yet that symbiotic relationship may have its origin and culminate in the very nature of the state itself. Of course the state's role is complex here:

> Its (criminal justice) language and procedure constantly announce to us that this is the form our collective, natural reason should take. It is, of course, also the most legitimate way in a modern society of levying violence against the disruptive, the dangerous, the inconvenient and the dissident.[8]

However if there is often – and perhaps inevitably – a subtext to the nomination of conduct as deviant in any given society, and an absence of dialogue about that code, there is quiescent in the public mind at least, a notion that in the course of utilizing the code against citizens, the state is conscious of certain individual rights. In other words there is a structure which lies between the nomination of deviance and the imposition of state punishment, which we call, and conceive of, as criminal *justice*.

That we trouble to call our system a just or due process one, that we aspire to hold certain rights dear, and that we regulate the confrontation between citizen and state which lies on 'the cutting edge of the abuse of power'[9] is axiomatic in our political and legal discourse and a product of our vision of what we are: a society conscious and cautious of individual liberties. Yet our understanding of what that caution is, is itself a product of our having named our system a 'due process' or 'fair procedure' one. The question arises as to how reflective that label is in the reality of the experience of those now caught within that system. Is there a gap between our aspirations and that reality? If so, are we caught between paying homage to certain ideals, while fashioning a structure or ideology more closely wedded to state needs? Is that solution one which relies on the limitations of language: the maintenance of a distance between what we say and what we do?

Colloquially, in Irish life, there is a tradition of 'living in translation'.[10] Part of this could be said to be attributable to our linguistic and political history: familiarity with a gap between words and their meaning, rules and their impact. But to what extent is it found reflected in the structure of our legal system? The Irish Constitution reveals more sombre and profound contradictions at the heart of the polity.[11] Article 2 declares: 'The national territory consists of the whole island of Ireland, its islands and the territorial seas', that is, 'the nation'. Article 3 declares 'the state':

> Pending the re-integration of the national territory, and without prejudice to the right of the Parliament and Government established by this Constitution to exercise

> jurisdiction over the whole of that territory, the laws
> enacted by that Parliament shall have . . . application
> as the laws of Saorstát Éireann . . .

Constitutions of course are meant to be largely aspirational documents, vagueness rather than precision characterizing their enumeration of our principles, the 'fundamentals' we hold dear in our society. Yet an obviously rather more disquieting dualism between what we aspire to and what we are, is found in another article containing potential for destruction or undercutting of those very values we espouse. Article 28.3.3 provides:

> Nothing in this Constitution shall be invoked to
> invalidate any law enacted by the Oireachtas which is
> expressed to be for the purpose of securing the public
> safety and the preservation of the State in time of war or
> armed rebellion, or to nullify any act done or purport-
> ing to be done in time of war or armed rebellion in
> pursuance of any such law. In this sub-section 'time of
> war' includes a time when . . . each of the Houses of
> the Oireachtas shall have resolved that . . . a national
> emergency exists . . . .

Ireland has been in such a 'state of emergency' since the 1970s and maintains a dual system of criminal justice, characterized by a non-jury court trying criminal cases (despite Article 38.5 provision that 'no person shall be tried on any criminal charge without a jury'), and extensive powers of detention following on arrest (s. 30 Offences Against the Person Act, 1939).[12] That we can with equanimity tolerate such a schizophrenic regime is perhaps due to the 'normalization' process which inevitably follows a familiarity with an emergency regime (or to a change in respect for or acceptance of the fundamental values of our Constitution). That we may fail to acknowledge or appreciate a change in those 'fundamental values' may be because we have already accepted what they have now become – in similar fashion to how they were once given to us (by the state)[13] – or rather that once the language remains the same we do not enquire too deeply into its meaning.

Rather disquietingly, therefore, it may be that our Constitution has fallen into disrepute because it is no longer reflective of the political or moral character of our state as we move towards a federation of Europe (an 'espaace judiciare éuropeène').[14] Yet to facilitate that process of integration we need to maintain our standing as a liberal democracy – with liberal rights and values somehow enshrined, if not respected. The Constitution has served admirably as proof of our state's adherence to those ideals. It has also cloaked the alternate regime which operates to deal with the repercussions of what is the longest running war in Europe.

The Irish legal system finds itself sharing traditions with the geographical and political giants on either side of our island shores: a common law adversarial tradition with England – distinct from the continental civil inquisitorial model – while our constitutional tradition shared with the United States, means that we more frequently look west, rather than east in citing jurisprudence in our courts.

Ideologically, morally, politically, Ireland seems caught in a quandary; straddling huge and powerful ideological divides and influences, while struggling to maintain the appearance of continuity, which has the dual advantage of facilitating acceptance, and concealing change. The scale of change amounts to a paradigm shift, forcing a crisis of identity or political morality in Ireland. Is there not something insidious, not to say fundamentally undemocratic and certainly dangerous, about a society that mutates without direction or discussion?

Crises are too often bought off with imminent and immediate, rather than considered responses. Too frequently are we reassured that such change can be accommodated with ease by our system, that the change is merely 'technical'. In such fashion the government gains the credence of doing something (or appearing to) while not fundamentally altering the kind of society we live in, or acknowledging its depth of crisis.

This tactic can be seen in the response of government to the perceived crime problem in the 1980s. The police at the time were using s. 30 (the 'extraordinary' provision) in relation to 'ordinary' crime. There was concern about the legality of such a practice,[15] and a call for greater police powers of arrest and detention to deal with the crime situation generally. The government responded with the Criminal Justice Act 1984, which provided for shorter periods of detention consequent on arrest,[16] thereby appearing to respond to the crime problem (without addressing any of the root causes of same), and yet reinforcing the 'due process' nature of our criminal justice system 'proper' or 'ordinary', by maintaining the distinction of the 'separate', 'extraordinary' regime to deal with 'terrorists'. The conundrum is complete: far from interfering with our adherence to liberal values, our extraordinary regime guarantees it.

We are not alone in this in Europe: the same sleight of hand was used by the British Government when in 1984, it introduced the Police and Criminal Evidence Act (PACE), with similar extended powers for the police, and changes in procedure. Once again very many of these reflect the kind of powers initially introduced by the 'extraordinary' regimen of the Prevention of Terrorism Act (PTA), introduced by the Labour government in 1974 in the aftermath of the Birmingham bombings (the definitive 'politics of the last atrocity' legislation). Although PACE could in many ways have accommodated the 'terrorist' regime under the PTA (aside from the 'exclusion orders' relevant only to those involved in Northern Ireland terrorism),[17] the two were kept distinct and in place, once again securing the public perception that something was being done while not initiating a crisis or debate as to what that change might infer.

More recent capitulation (of our 'core' values) and accommodation (of change) within our criminal justice system in Ireland, has been manifest in the wake of other political crises. The Lavinia Kerwick case[18] is typical of the rash of concern surrounding certain kinds of offences, those involving sexual violence against women and children in particular. Here again the government has appeared to respond to public demands for action with alacrity and relative ease. Schooled in the process of legislating a response, the government introduces and passes bills with a degree of ease and consensus which can only indicate that either the changes are long overdue, or warranted, or do not pose any fundamental problems for our collective consciences. The public – lulled into the security of law as a panacea for political reform – appears to be satiated by the legislative response. Few ask the awkward questions as to what other social, economic, or political responses might be appropriate. None query how the structure that is our criminal law copes with these incursions. It is that last question I wish to pose, for it may well be that the high moral authority with which we have in the past castigated the British justice system conceals a nervousness about the quality of our own which is indeed warranted by the reality. It may also be that the register in which we respond to crises within our society is out of synch with the base or fundamental values we espouse in our Constitution.

If so, then we are a society operating a duality at the very core of our state. Since the repressive regime of the eighteenth century, a lot has changed in criminal justice but it should not be forgotten that the origins of this structure are bloody: the legacy it left, a commitment to a recognition of the unequal nature of that balance between citizen and state. Change in that equation may mean that that place where the individual citizen risks most, may well be a perilous place for any of us to be.

3. THE TRIAL

Cut up sorrow in inches, weigh content
You can weigh John Brown's body well enough
But how and in what balance can you weigh John Brown?[19]

The ostensible focal point of the criminal justice system is the trial. Though many might argue that currently the more immediate and intimate confrontation takes place on the street, the trial remains the most visible portion of the criminal process, to the extent that it is regulated and recorded (a phenomenon now increasingly characteristic of the pre-trial interrogation process).

An appreciation of the limitations of the trial is best gleaned from focusing on its human dimension, for within our system it is the people (as witnesses, jurors etc.) who although not *central* to the event, i.e. not accused or prosecutor or even victim, whose involvement dictates how that process runs. This is a consequence or product of a process that is largely *testimonial* and *oral* in its tradition.

In a piece entitled 'The Locked Room' in the *New York Trilogy*, Paul Auster states that 'stories happen only to those who are able to tell them.'[20] Our legal process is continually engaged in the telling of stories – the stories of witnesses and what happened to them, or what they saw, or think, is a fact familiar to lawyers and to the public at large who then engage with those stories (and their retelling) through the media, through situation-dramas and through their own real life experiences. Like the seanachaí, those who reconstruct and tell stories – each time a little different from the last – inject them with their particular perspective. That is the meat and trade of lawyers and explains the relative equanimity with which they regard such telling or retelling within the context of the concepts of truth and justice. That is not to say that lawyers – or judges – are jaundiced when it comes to those concepts, but simply that they are aware of how relative they are. So it is that the ultimate reconstruction of a tale – by the court – is readily recognizable as the result of a crude process where both parties fight as hard as they can, in as biased a way as they can, to present their side of the story to the court. The court does not engage in any investigation of its own and what will , emerge is perhaps as close an approximation of what occurred as can be achieved, given the limitations of time, money and human recollection.

The court finds itself not fashioning an accurate account, but one that is satisfactory in terms of its compliance with a set of values. The process is undeniably unscientific and reflective of our ultimate desire to 'do justice' as we see it. Such a system accommodates the presumption of innocence and the preference that nine guilty go free rather than one innocent be convicted. It is entirely different from the inquisitorial model of justice favoured by continental European countries for example, where the court takes an active investigative role and the process is not rooted in a belief in the value of orality (or testimonial evidence) or the power of cross-examination as testament to truth. The latter are typical of jurisdictions operating accusatorial systems under the common law – England, Ireland and the US being amongst them.

PROBLEMS OF LEGAL ADJUDICATION, EVIDENCE, EXPERT WITNESSES, JURIES

The task that is presented to a criminal court is that on the evidence (comprising that information which is presented in court) a decision be made; specifically that of the innocence or guilt of those accused of a specified crime. That information is piecemeal in nature – not only because it consists in the main of retrospective reconstructions of past events on the part of biased protagonists, but also because of rules regarding admissibility of evidence which operate to exclude otherwise relevant and probative information. This exclusion is partly a function of the limitations of human beings – witnesses and jurors – and partly a product of more overt policy considerations. Whatever the specific rationale, the signals given to society by this procedure reflect a commitment to principles – most particularly those placing limitations on state incursion on individual rights. That commitment has a history.

Douglas Hay has written of the value of 'formalism' in the eighteenth-century criminal justice regime: it assured people of its veracity.[21] Thompson illustrates this phenomenon with the rather grisly epithet of those being executed spending their final breath on procedure.

> On the gallows men would actually complain, in their
> 'last dying words', if they felt that in some particular the
> due forms of law had not been undergone.[22]

The rationale of adherence to procedure is wedded to the nature of the relationship between individual and state. What needs to be queried is the extent to which that we pay homage to is realized in the experience of those caught within the criminal justice system (the accused) and the degree to which our assessment of that process is reflective of a 'learned' view of what is acceptable. Various factors come into play here: the image the state portrays of itself; the perception of fear on the part of the public (crime: the likelihood of being a victim or accused); and the manner in which public policy issues are conveyed and portrayed (the media) which may dictate the form of response.

If one is not to fall foul of other equally powerful assumptions one must be wary of all manner of influence and presumption: not just the 'truths' held currently to be self-evident by politicians or the public, but also those propounded by lawyers or critics. Twining characterized the magnitude of that task thus:

> to examine critically the underlying assumptions of all
> legal discourse and to question established ways of

> thought, especially those that are becoming entrenched
> . . . to pick away at all assumptions, including (one's)
> own. Whether (one) adopts the role of . . . the child in
> the story of the emperor's clothes or any other form of
> hired subversive (the) first job is to ask questions and
> with the greatest respect to the greatest of our gurus to
> let the consequences take care of themselves.[23]

With this edict in mind, I propose to look at some of those features of our criminal justice which are characteristic of the way in which we conduct such legal adjudication.

THE JURY

Central to the adversarial system, particularly in the criminal context, is the adjudicative or fact-finding role of the jury: they determine the ultimate issue of guilt or innocence at trial. The jury make that determination based on the admissible evidence presented by counsel for either side, and the instruction on the law delivered by the trial judge. Much of the argument (and effect) of the trial turns on how successful counsel from either side may be in getting evidence before the court, or excluding it from perusal. Many of the reasons why the jury may not get to see apparently probative and relevant evidence are due to policy considerations or social values: for example however reliable a confession, we would not admit it if it had been obtained by torture, a practice of which we do not approve. However, evidence may also be excluded because of a belief in the frailty of human cognition, specifically that of the jury. Examples would include a failure to appreciate the inaccuracy of hearsay evidence (i.e. evidence of what someone else had told the witness); overestimation of the value of visual identification evidence *or* evidence of the accused's past bad behaviour. The function of many of these rules has been described as that of attempting to control a bunch of ignorant illiterates – to wit the jury.[24] It could, of course, be argued that today's juror is a much more sophisticated animal; able to make such judgements and appreciate subtleties. Alternatively it could be argued that society has developed to such an extent that we all know much more about less, so that the role of the jury is an anachronism which has been superceded by the growth of expertise. It is this latter argument which has come to the fore in the context of the recent proliferation of expertise and experts who appear in our courts. Even in the most mundane cases, for instance a simple 'running down' action, one is forced to face the spectre of trial by expert (engineer, psychologist, psychiatrist etc.). Expert witnesses appear so valuable that we may feel they should replace the jury, i.e. we have reached a state of knowledge in society where we no longer 'need' the common input, or that they supplant the jury anyway, making the latter superfluous as they simply cede to the expert in any event.

If one regrets the loss of the jury as part of the process of adjudication, one finds oneself defending it, yet on what basis? Because it is marginally more sophisticated or at least more democratic than some of its predecessors – trial by ordeal or trial by water? That we are numbered amongst a limited number of jurisdictions operating such a system, including the United States? That it is part of our rights and duties as citizens? That we don't trust judges? That we trust our fellow citizens?

The latter stance begs the question as to who is our fellow citizen?[25] Currently in the United States jurors are the product of an elaborate process called the 'voir dire', where defence and state use their pre-emptory challenges, and challenges for cause, to eliminate those jurors whom 'experts' advise will not be favourable to their position. The procedure in this jurisdiction is less sophisticated or scientific and much shorter, counsel for either side having to make relatively quick decisions on the basis of minimal and superficial (not to say stereotypical) assessments. For instance in rape trials, one of the recurring criticisms of women's groups was the overwhelmingly 'male' composition of juries. Concern about the composition of juries in this and other jurisdictions is evident from the recommendation of the Irish Government's Advisory Committee on Fraud[26] that pre-emptory challenges (i.e. automatic challenges) be abolished, and that of the British Royal Commission on Criminal Justice that consideration be taken of the racial or ethnic composition of juries in criminal trials.[27] Racial make-up became an issue in the first (and second) 'Rodney King' trials in the United States, where it was seen to be a factor closely tied to the acceptability of the verdict.[28]

Are we then moving closer to or away from adjudication by one's peers? What of the argument that anyone who is not clever enough to get out of jury service, or stupid enough to be caught should not be on a jury anyway? The process of excusing oneself from jury service is arguably too easily and too readily utilized by certain classes in our society.

In the state of Florida jury selection is made from the electoral register, and since many do not register to vote precisely to avoid jury duty, the pool is said to be mostly republican and as older, retired people tend to be available, juries seem to the eye aged, and predominantly female. Moreover many are 'practised' jurors and have been called over and over again. An elaborate process of 'video instruction' is given to members of the jury prior to their selection which calls repeatedly on jurors to use their common sense. (One could argue the same 'common sense' approach is being used over and over again.) The image of the leading proponent of jury trial exhorting its citizens to use their 'common sense' as the sole justification for that system, is not exactly inspiring.[29] It is questionable, at the very least, whether the number of citizens participating in jury service in Florida and other jurisdictions are representative of ethnic/class groups, and to what extent that system is currently providing either an exercise in participatory democracy *or* education of its citizens in the manner of adjudication in their courts.

Other vulnerabilities of the jury system may become evident once one examines it with a more critical eye. A jury is said to be a judgement by one's peers: the value or merit being an assessment by people who appreciate the context of the conduct and its assessment. Yet a jury can also be reflective of community values or judgements in a manner which is too much rooted in that society's sense of outrage, rather than their deliberation on the evidence before them. How valuable then is that process: is it merely expressive of societal outrage or is it that far removed from a lynching? In the United States where first amendment rights and the guarantee of free speech rank way up the hierarchy of rights, jury interviewing (amongst other considerable commentary on the trial process and proceedings which would be unfamiliar to Irish audiences) is a practice routinely engaged in. In Ireland such would certainly be frowned upon. However as a young lawyer I was once impressed upon to go and talk to jury members in the aftermath of a trial of an individual for offences relating to rioting on Spike Island, at the time used to 'house' convicted 'joyriding' offenders from Dublin.

The evidence against the accused, consisted solely of visual identification by two prison wardens, the incident having taken place at night amidst some chaos. The trial judge issued a strong warning to the jury as to the dangers of convicting solely on such evidence. Nonetheless the jury stayed out a considerable length of time adjudicating their verdict. Their reason was that they felt it would be terrible if nobody paid for what happened on Spike Island.

It may similarly be questionable if the jury in some cases can focus on what they are asked to do in that case (serve justice) rather than on what is going to happen if they do. Mindful of the earlier riots which led to over fifty deaths and a billion dollars in damage in the aftermath of the first King verdict, jurors in the federal case might have difficulty in separating the two. With this in mind meticulous precautions were taken to call an impartial jury. Notices were sent to 6,000 prospective jurors in Los Angeles, of whom only 333 were willing to be sequestered for two months. They had to complete a fifty-three-page questionnaire. Despite this, some remained sceptical of the feasibility of their task: Stephen Scaring, a prominent criminal defense lawyer in New York, was quoted in the *New York Times* as stating: 'They know the community wants a certain verdict in this case. . . . The media, public officials, the general population all want a verdict of guilty and nothing else. I think that's a frightening situation in a free country.'[30]

Despite all the difficulties that emerge when one considers the actual as opposed to the ostensible value of the jury system, is there some merit in the involvement of the *citizen* in the process of legal adjudication? It is hard to conceive of a more direct or immediate way in which (other) individuals can have an input into how the state treats its citizens. That the immediacy and access may on occasion be invoked to contrary effect is part of the 'dialogue' where jurors have given expression to their feelings.

The 'perverse' or contrary verdict of a jury (e.g. *Morgantaler* in Canada and *Clive Ponting* in England)[31] is a phenomenon with a history and some would contend a very great value. Thompson finds its value in the context of the eighteenth-century regime of the draconian 'Black Act', which provides an object lesson in how valuable the 'brake' of the jury system may sometimes be.[32] The 'Black Act' gave unprecedented legal power to those who had a direct and personal interest in the conviction of men who were a nuisance to them. Thompson comments that 'It was a power which made nonsense of a whole costly historical paraphernalia whose proclaimed object was to safeguard the liberty of the subject.' Yet the traditional safeguard of the jury system remained, and in the acquittal of one John Huntridge by twelve men Thompson finds a check to the growth of arbitrary power:

> 'Men will, on occasion, act not according to their own interests, but according to the expectations and values attached to a certain role. The role of juror carried (and still carries) such an inheritance of expectations.

> The acquittal of Huntridge may have been more important than a score of more celebrated cases in defending the subject against the state.'

LEGISLATIVE DEVELOPMENTS

Article 38.5 of the Irish Constitution guarantees a right to trial by jury in criminal matters which are not 'minor' *or* where the administration of justice and the preservation of public peace and order cannot be secured effectively by the ordinary courts. (The third exception relates to military offences.) The fragility of that guarantee can be seen in the most recent proposal in the Criminal Justice (Public Order) Bill 1993 (presented by the Minister for Justice on 25 June 1993) that in relation to offences under s. 20 of that bill, the automatic entitlement to opt for jury trial be removed.

Section 20 deals with assault or obstruction of a peace officer meriting on summary conviction £1,000 fine or twelve months imprisonment or both and on conviction or indictment a fine or imprisonment for up to five years or both. The change is specific: limited to that particular offence – even in a bill committed to a plethora of wide-ranging and widely defined offences of a public order nature. It is the first obvious chink in the armour of the jury trial and arguably *the* most significant element in this piece of (particularly draconian) legislation.

An interesting contrast with this proposal is found in the recommendations of the Government Advisory Committee on Fraud presented in December 1992.[33] The committee was conscious in its inquiry of 'the constraints created by the provisions of . . . the Irish Constitution and the requirements of natural justice and fair procedures'. They noted in particular that the constitutional guarantee (Article 38.5) of trial by jury does not permit an exception for departure from same in the context of serious fraud, and comments:

If this were not the case, we would certainly have considered whether the interests of justice would better be
served by the trial of serious fraud offences before one
or more judges advised by expert assessors. It is clear
that a serious fraud trial can place an enormous burden
on jurors, who can be taken from their homes or jobs
for weeks, perhaps months on end and are expected,
with no specialist knowledge or training, to absorb and
make sense of complex and technical evidence of a
sustained intensity that few will have previously
experienced.[34]

Their respect for the centrality of jury trial is further reflected in
their consideration of the inclusion of one or more jurors from a
specialist panel in such cases, which they felt would fall foul of the
criteria of *representativeness* established by the Supreme Court in *de
Burca* v *AG*. Significantly, they then turned their attention to the
peremptory challenge, i.e. the right to veto absolutely and without
question the selection of a juror: seven currently available to prosecution and each defendant. The committee noted these were felt to
be particularly valuable to defendants, giving a feeling of control and
confidence justice will be done. Unconvinced of the latter (but
sufficiently solicitous of the accused to take them on board for consideration) they recommend the abolition of the pre-emptory challenge:

It's availability to both sides in a criminal trial inevitably
encourages its use as a tactical device in the selection of
jurors who on the basis of the clothes they wear or the
newspapers they carry are thought to be favourable to
one side or the other. In our view, fairness in a jury can
best be ensured by genuine random selection subject
to strict criteria of disqualification and the right of
objection for cause shown.[35]

Given the context of serious fraud trials – seen to be part of the criminal law needing attention,[36] it is interesting to note the respect being shown for such a traditional element of our adversarial criminal justice system: one which poses particular difficulty for prosecutor and juror in complex fraud cases. This solicitude is found wanting in the Criminal Justice (Public Order) Bill's provisions. One is tempted to question if it is the context – the particular criminal activity – that is significant. This piecemeal approach is also found in the Criminal Evidence Act 1992 provision for witnesses in certain criminal cases.[37] In the recent bill it indicates a rather less savoury concern for the rights of those perpetrators of 'white collar' crimes, absent for those likely to be involved in the conduct governed by the Public Order Bill's provisions.

It is tempting to recall the statement of Senator O'Toole in the Seanad on the latter kind of provision:

> Successive governments and educational systems have reinforced inequity, have consolidated disadvantage and have ensured the continuation of underprivilege with the result that the people sentenced to prison largely come from the same social class and same areas. *It sometimes strikes me it might be cheaper to build walls around some of our disadvantaged areas than maintaining our prisons.*[38]

THE VALUE OF PROCEDURE

The judiciary of course generally defend the jury system by reference to constitutional values, and there is no doubt that in Ireland despite (or because of) the aberration of the Special Criminal Court, juries are perceived as an integral part of the legal system and culture. There is a belief amongst lawyers in the value of formality or procedure and the maintainance (and validity) of institutions. Most lawyers have bought Frankfurters line in *McNabb*[39] that the history of liberty is the history of procedural safeguards. Yet if one follows up Twining's invitation to further question that belief and its basis, one has to acknowledge that Packers' concept of fair procedure 'due process' is well known to be that which the judges tell us it is.[40] Anyone who has watched the vacillation of the US courts since *Miranda*[41] in terms of the exclusion of illegally obtained evidence, or the Irish decisions on improper police behaviour in the obtaining of evidence since *O'Brien*,[42] knows that and is familiar with the demonstrated elasticity of either of those formulae.

It is a similar tale in the English context, with the uncertainty surrounding the court's interpretation and application of s. 78 of the Police and Criminal Evidence Act,[43] which exhorts the courts to have regard to how the evidence in a case was obtained. The Canadian courts have also demonstrated that the particular provision in their Charter dealing with unlawfully obtained evidence (s. 24(2))[44] does not inspire belief as to its substantive content or worth. These are indeed 'moveable feasts' determined by the judiciary. This is characteristic of interpretation (by the judiciary of law) which is a *creative* function – particularly encouraged by 'constitutional rights' which tend to provide only broad background strokes, leaving the judiciary to fill in the detail of the picture. The other side of that of course is that a citizen going to that Charter or document alone, cannot interpret it or its position on his/her rights. Yet what of the process itself – the 'going through the motions' by the citizen – lawyer at her side to invoke, read and argue the rules? Is there at least a notional equality then – a value in the visibility of the fight? That there might well be is illustrated by comparison with recent 'alternative developments' and their implications for individuals.

In 'family law' for instance, the area of mediation, conciliation or arbitration has developed and at times supercedes the legal process: it has been widely viewed as more 'user friendly', appropriate, even more feminist for these domestic issues. Not only does this

received a substantial degree of public support which was reflective of the public perception that the system does not work, or does not deliver justice. The Government's response was to produce a bill[46] providing for state appeals against sentence (already available under law, but appearance is everything), the admissibility of 'victim impact statements' as relevant to sentencing, and awards of compensation to the victim in the context of such a criminal trial. This bill received a second metamorphosis after a change of government, and became law in May 1993, following 'hot on foot' of the recently passed Criminal Evidence Act 1992,[47] which was introduced in January 1992, passed and brought into effect within six months, making sweeping changes to our criminal justice system. It facilitated the admissibility of documentary evidence (previously hampered by the hearsay rule which insisted on oral testimony by a witness), and eased the task of testifying on the part of certain witnesses – primarily those victims of violent or sexual assaults. These changes were at once offered as a panacea, or at least partial solution, to the problem of white-collar crime or fraud, and sexual abuse or violence against women and children respectively – while their impact on the nature of our system of legal adjudication was studiously ignored. All of this occurred against the background of rather vocal criticism of the British criminal justice system evidenced by *causes célèbres* like the Birmingham Six, Guilford Four and Winchester Three. (Conveniently forgotten seemed to be the other significant 'number' case of the Tallaght Two, or the Christopher Lynch, or Nicky Kelly débâcles within our own jurisdiction.)[48]

Ireland is not alone in accommodating a certain degree of collective myopia in relation to a conflict between declarations of principle and practice. The second trial involving the police officers accused of violating Rodney King's civil rights in the United States[49] illustrated how a separate set of federal proceedings arising out of the same incident and in the aftermath of an initial acquittal by a jury were employed. Despite concerns regarding jury composition etc., the phenomenon of accommodating a second adjudication of the same accuseds in relation to the same incident (albeit a distinct charge), sits uncomfortably (or should) with principles of double-jeopardy, trial by jury and the finality of verdicts. [50]

If we in Ireland have a mechanism for doing justice, wedded to certain ideals (principles of double jeopardy, orality, cross-examination, confrontation, due process) how can that justice system accommodate change without crisis?

THE ROLE OF THE MEDIA

It is only in our culture's (Irish as well as US) capitulation to the collective confession, through the media (and in particular the new despots – talk show hosts – the Gerry Ryan and Rush Limbaughs of this world)[51] that we find evidence of crisis. There is a change in public perception, that something is wrong or must be accounted for, or at least explained. Lavinia Kerwick first spoke of her dissatisfaction on the Gerry Ryan show; the Rodney King controversy was characterized by repeated airings of the video of police officers beating King on American television, as politicians of all political hues rushed to comment on the verdict and trial.

We only hear of the detail, never the entire picture. The public confessional phenomenon – the media exposé – stark, immediate and limited in effect, initiates a similar response (legislatively) and is particularly vulnerable to 'the politics of the last atrocity'.

Since the media – written, visual and aural – has been central to the elucidation and resolution (if not creation in the sense of representation) of the 'events' in Irish life which have led to current political and hence legislative action, it would be foolhardy – if not neglectful – not to address its increasing role in the context of criminal law reform. Each of us (particularly those of us de-sensitized to the constant presence of Northern Ireland related violence) has become accustomed to 'the mundane presence of images of crime at many moments of our lives'.[52] For many of us still (despite the 'lip-service' paid to the reality of crime in our lives) it is where we come in contact with the 'criminal' world. Once again the manner in which we acquire that knowledge is significant.

Sparks elucidates that format for us:

> Such images, however familiar and routinized they may be in the way they enter our domestic spaces, are never self-evident in either meaning or effect. They are co-ordinated in stories and discourses of particular kinds. They demonstrate particular preoccupations. They postulate problems, explanations and resolutions. They invite certain responses, often in ways which are difficult to refuse . . . It is also interesting and important to wonder what consequences follow for a culture which builds into its routine forms of communication and exchange, and its representations of itself to its members, such an abiding preoccupation with crime, law and punishment, organized in a particular and characteristic moral structure.[53]

Once again it is the form and the structure of the dialogue which is vital here. The way in which we (and our legislators) react to *perceived* crises is dictated by the manner of their telling.

The role of the media in terms of reportage of incidents and public response is therefore of importance. In a very real sense it is more than just the disseminator of information: it is the creator of a response. In connecting the private 'domestic' world of people's experience with the public world of crime, it sets the agenda for interpretation, response and criminal law reform. A dialogue between state and public is essential on the issue of the criminal justice system. In a very real sense they are mutually dependent and definitional. This is why control of that encounter is vital. Great difficulties emerge however once you realize the conveyor of information and of the expression of public opinion, is also the purveyor of fact and *fiction* – about crime – in a given format. An interesting contrast can be drawn between what is demanded of us as spectators to the portrayal of crime (fact or fiction) on our television sets and the spectacle created for us by Sophocles, where the dilemma of individual and state is manifest in the character of Antigone. Creon, representative of current state power, order and law, gives the classic statement of the individual's sub-servience to the state:

> Creon: Of course you cannot know a man completely,
> his character, his principles, sense of judgement,
> not till he's shown his colours, ruling the people,
> making laws. Experience, there's the test.
> As I see it, whoever assumes the task,
> the awesome task of setting the city's course,
> and refuses to adopt the soundest policies
> but fearing someone, keeps his lips locked tight,
> he's utterly worthless. So I rate him now,
> I always have. And whoever places a friend
> above the good of his own country, he is nothing:
> I have no use for him. Zeus my witness,
> Zeus who sees all things, always –
> . . . But whoever proves his loyalty to the state –
> I'll prize that man in death as well as life.[54]

Sophocles demands more than our reaction. He asks us to think, and in the character of Antigone gives expression to the dilemma of a claim to a higher authority, a challenge to the positivist law of the state:

> Creon: And still you had the gall to break this law?
> Antigone: Of course I did. It wasn't Zeus, not in the
> least, who made this proclamation – not to me.
> Nor did that Justice, dwelling with the gods

beneath the earth, ordain such laws for men.
Nor did I think your edict had such force
that you, a mere mortal, could override the gods,
the great unwritten, unshakable traditions.
They are alive, not just today or yesterday:
they live forever, from the first of time,
and no one knows when they first saw the light.
These laws – I was not about to break them,
not out of fear of some man's wounded pride,
and face the retribution of the gods.
. . . And if my present actions strike you as foolish,
let's just say I've been accused of folly
by a fool.[55]

Is it worthwhile considering whether Antigone's voice (that of dissent: the deviant) is one heard in the purview of recent information about 'crisis' in our Irish criminal justice system? Did we for instance hear the voice of William Conry or the Kilkenny incest victim's father?[56] Did we want to?

5. THE SEARCH FOR NORMS

THE INEVITABILITY OF LEGISLATIVE AND JUDICIAL CLASH

That something is 'amiss' within our criminal justice system is a view held with a remarkable degree of unanimity by our legislators; that it is related to and can be mitigated by adjustment in procedure or process meets with similar consensus. That there is not any necessary correlation between the process that is there, and some higher principles, is a view which while not given expression, would seem implicitly accepted. What then are the influences informing the legislative responses to the crisis in Irish criminal justice?

LEGISLATIVE ASSUMPTIONS

While those influences do not present themselves as a whole, there is however a sum of their parts – statements, truths or assumptions found to lie behind the political debate surrounding reform in this area.[57] In large measure they would seem to comprise the following:

Crime is on the increase and that is bad

Victim support organizations are good

We need to change our criminal justice system

Procedure/technicalities are bad

Media reporting is good

Victim-orientated systems are good

Adversarial systems are bad

Convictions are good

Acquitting the guilty is bad

Victim impact statements will lead to heavier sentencing

Victims should be compensated

Judges need training; judicial attitudes are bad

Women and children are victims (and so good)

Accuseds (male) are guilty and so bad

While some would quibble with the extent to which the above are singly or together reflective of any particular consensus, there is no doubt some of their number reflect the policy choices made in the Criminal Evidence Act 1992 and the Criminal Justice Act 1993. Moreover the tenor of the debate and commentary is *never* without a context, never without a particular crime. Rarely is there a call for a more general debate. But if these influences do not gel with traditional 'general principles' of criminal law, do they reflect an overall change in approach? One that counters that some accuseds are different, or that some crimes need to be treated distinctly, or that some victims are more meritorious? If so, does this lead to a distinct criminal regime *or* merely and adjustment to general principle?

CRIMINAL EVIDENCE ACT 1992

The Criminal Evidence Act 1992 illustrates this legislative myopia. The Act deals with only three areas of criminal procedure: documentary evidence, the giving of testimony by witnesses in certain proceedings (sexual and violent offences) and the competence and compellability of spouses as prosecution witnesses. There is no apparent connection between these three areas of procedure. It is the former two which prove most controversial. They also share an interesting and inherent contradiction in how they are to be invoked by the judiciary. Part II deals with documentary evidence. Traditionally excluded by the 'hearsay rule' which preferred the oral testimony of a witness in court, it is now admissible in certain circumstances. The reason for the change – that records are now reliable, and important decisions made on them daily. What this ignores is the fact that reliability or authenticity was never the sole rationale for the hearsay rule. Part of it lay in the desirability of subjecting the declarant to cross-examination under oath. The jury's assessment of the value of that evidence was firmly located in their assessment of the witness' demeanour. Indeed the Act itself invokes criteria other than authenticity and reliability, empowering the judiciary to exclude documents if their admission would result in *unfairness to the accused*. What if that very concept were to necessitate viva voce evidence and cross-examination? Similarly Part III of the Act which concerns the elicitation of testimony from witnesses in certain proceedings introduces changes in procedure far removed from traditional methods of viva voce testimony, cross-examination etc. Evidence can be given by live television link, through an intermediary or by means of video-recording in certain circumstances. When? Again when the judiciary feel it would be in the *interests of justice* to do so, a component part of which is *fairness to the accused*.

The conundrum is complete: the assumption that there is not a necessary and prior correlation between what is already *there* in terms of procedure, and fairness to the accused. Why then (if the latter is the case) can that not be said generally? Are the distinctions kept between separate covers for fear that comparison between their contexts would lead us to see another significance in the different processes – public order defendants meriting jury trial less frequently than their white collar cohorts? Certainly the legislators seem loath to acknowledge or expound on the general nature of the change.

JUDICIAL CONCEPT OF 'FAIR PROCEDURE'

Only the judiciary seem to struggle to accommodate change within norms. Indeed the legislators – at least in the context of the Criminal Evidence Act 1992 – cede to them that task, asking them to operate the changes 'in accordance with the 'interests of justice' or 'fairness to the accused'. Of course the judiciary do have a concept of what is 'fair' or what is 'just'. It is somewhat malleable (and so the worth of our constitutional or 'core' values problematic), but at least the question is asked, the accommodation made.

Side by side with the pointillist picture being dictated by politics, not so far removed from the 'parish pump', is a broader agenda being blocked in constitutionally, judicially and hence legally. If one takes a look at recent Irish judicial statements from the bench, a picture emerges of the very polar opposite of 'piecemeal' reform, with the Irish judiciary straining to give procedures and rights a 'common habitat and name'. These same protagonists are charged with 'melting' the two together. The judiciary are well equipped as can be seen by their approach to the elucidation of what is meant by 'fair procedure'. It is interesting to consider judicial comments emanating from the bench during the same period as that which gave birth to current and proposed legislation aimed at adjustments to criminal procedure.

In the context of the decision of the Court of Criminal Appeal in *DPP* v *T* (1988)[59] which secured the competence of a spouse to testify in the context of charges of sexual abuse by a father of his child, Judge Walsh declared that the common law rule impeding such testimony was contrary to and negated by the Constitution: 'The administration of justice itself requires the public has a right to every man's evidence'. He referred to *Murphy* v *Dublin Corporation* (1972)[60] which held that in the last resort the decision must be that of the court:

> The exercise of the judicial power carried with it the power to compel the attendance of witnesses, the production of evidence and *a fortiori* the answering of questions by the witness. This is the ultimate safeguard of justice in the state whether it be in pursuit of the guilty or vindication of the innocent.

Sometimes the judiciary's concept of 'fair process' has led them to reject some traditional common law rules of evidence. Take for example the statement of Judge Hederman in *McGrail* (1989)[61] abandoning the previous common law rule inhibiting accused persons from attacking prosecution witnesses:

> . . . the principles of fair procedure must apply. A procedure which inhibits the accused from challenging the veracity of the evidence against him at the risk of having his own previous character put in evidence is not a fair procedure.

In *DPP* v *O'Reilly* (1990)[62] one finds a similar endorsement of fair procedure, and a view of what that might comprise.

Judge O'Flaherty delivering the judgement of the Court referred to the judgement of Chief Justice O'Higgins in *State (Healy)* v *Donoghue* (1976)[63] to the effect:

> In the first place the concept of justice which is specifically referred to in the preamble (to the Constitution) in relation to the freedom and dignity of

the individual appears again in the provisions of Article 34 which deals with the courts. It is justice which is to be administered in the courts and this concept of justice must import not only fairness and fair procedure but also regard to the dignity of the individual.

The fact finding role of a jury at trial, in terms of its centrality to the process, is also endorsed by the view that appellate courts should be slow to interfere as that finding is made on the basis of physically seeing and hearing witnesses and not simply receiving their testimony in documentary form. Judge McCarthy in *DPP* v *Egan* (1990)[64] stated:

> In reading the record of the evidence the appellate court cannot assess the credibility of witnesses nor the cogency of evidence of primary facts or of inference of fact which are dependent on credibility of a witness or witnesses.

(Again in the State of Florida Criminal Courts the trial judge instructs the jury that they should make the finding as to the credibility of witnesses not only on the basis of what they say but on their general demeanour.)

In *O'Leary* v *AG* (1990)[65] Judge Costello finds the presumption of innocence, part of the common law prior to 1937, to have been for so long a postulate of every criminal trial, that a criminal trial held otherwise is prima facie not held in due course of law. Of course Judge Costello then goes on to state that in certain circumstances the Oireachtas can restrict the exercise of such a right, which is not absolute. It is interesting however, that in finding the provisions before him not to be contrary to such a presumption, despite their 'reverse-onus' character, (placing the burden of proof on the accused), he has to go through a series of mental and verbal gyrations, which from one perspective only serve to endorse how fundamental he must perceive these principles to be.

In *Mapp* v *Gilhooley* (1991)[66] a decision concerned with the necessity of swearing a child in a civil case, led to Chief Justice Finlay stating that it was a fundamental principle of the common law in criminal or civil trials that viva voce (oral) evidence must be given on oath or affirmation. *DPP* v *Kehoe* (1991)[67] is an interesting decision concerned with the role of the jury, and their potential over-shadowing by an expert. In this case the expert had testified that the accused, who was mounting a defence of provocation, did not have the intent to kill and was telling the truth. Judge O'Flaherty delivering the judgement of the court stated:

> The court is of opinion that the accused's defence was properly to be considered by the jury without such elaboration and that further in the course of his evidence it is clear that Dr Behan overstepped the mark . . . These are clearly matters four square within the jury's function and a witness no more than the trial judge or anyone else is not entitled to trespass on what is the jury's function.

A later comment is interesting for its endorsement – and faith – in the jurors' role, rather than that of the trial judge. This is particularly significant in a jurisdiction where judicial charges to the jury on matters of law, are largely unbridled and a matter of judicial discretion. This latter can be exercised very powerfully, without ever overstepping the mark, and matters of inflection, tone of voice and intonation, cannot be devined from transcripts. In the United States, by contrast, instruction by the trial judge to the jury is taken from a composite code. It is simply a statement of the law and reiteration of relevant principles (also contained in the code) such as are felt to be necessary by the trial judge, and agreed before charging, with counsel on either side: an entirely different process mandating in a very pragmatic way the central role of the jury, and the limited input from the bench. Judge O'Flaherty may be found to be placing a 'judicial' (as opposed to legislative) brake on the judicial role in this area:

> Increasingly, it is the experience in this jurisdiction as in other jurisdictions that a trial judge abstains from offering any view of the evidence, good bad or indifferent. That is not to say that trial judges are not entitled to offer a view but more and more trial judges consider that *juries are best left to see evidence through a glass clearly rather than to have it either magnified or diminished by the judge's intervention*.

In *Goodman* (1991)[68] Judge McCarthy stated that common law rights were obscured by the Constitutional guarantee of fundamental rights:

> The prescripts of natural justice – to hear the other side and not to be a judge in one's own cause, have themselves been subsumed by the constitutional right to fair procedures. The right to be heard incorporates the right to be put to answer, to be told of the allegation, and to confront the witnesss. History may well be a guide but only a guide to constitutional construction. Rights are to be found within the constitutional framework, some created, others identified and guaranteed.

Chief Justice Finlay in that same case noted that it had been submitted on the part of the applicants that the nature of the resolutions coupled with the inquisitorial nature of the Tribunal, constituted a failure by the state and its laws to protect and vindicate the good name and property rights of the applicants. It was further submitted that the procedural deficiencies of the Tribunal, amounted to a want of due process or fair procedure contrary to Article 40.3 of the Constitution. In distinguishing between the Tribunal proceedings, which he characterizes as 'a simple fact-finding operation' and a criminal trial, Chief Justice Finlay rejected the submission made, but accepted the proposition that a guarantee of fair procedure is a part of Article 40.3.

In so doing however, he made some interesting comments about criminal trials and Article 38:

> The essential ingredient of a trial of a criminal offence in our law, which is indivisible from any other ingredient, is that it is heard before a court or judge which has got the power to punish in the event of a verdict of guilty. It is of the *essence* of a trial on a *criminal charge* or a trial on a criminal offence that the proceedings are *accusatorial*, involving a prosecutor and an accused, and that the sole purpose and object of the verdict be it one of acquittal or conviction, is to form the base for either a discharge of the accused from the jeopardy in which he stood in the case of an acquittal, or for his punishment for the crime which he has committed in the case of a conviction.

The strongest statement to date however, on the philosophy behind constitutional 'due process' and the role of procedure is undoubtedly that of the Supreme Court in *Kenny* (1990).[69] In a pragmatic sense it also led to the jettisoning of 'real' evidence, in the form of drugs undoubtedly found on the accused's premises, and invalidated a procedure for the obtaining of warrants used by the Gardai for over thirty years, on the basis of which thousands of warrants had been issued, and searches carried out.

Interestingly, the Supreme Court specifically referred to the American Supreme court decision of *US* v *Leon* which in introducing the 'good faith' exception to the *Miranda* ruling, wounded (in some view mortally) the American exclusionary rule, in its sanitizing of any police (mis)behaviour carried out in 'good faith'. While a previous line of decisions by the Irish courts had similarly seemed to allow for a 'green Garda' exception to the exclusionary rule (particularly in confession cases), these were now subsumed by a Supreme court decision in the context of the 'harsher' world of real evidence, which existence cannot be denied.[70]

The decision in *Kenny* is firmly located in a principled or 'biased' view of the criminal justice system and its role. Chief Justice Finlay delivering the majority judgement notes the precedent where he and Judge McCarthy in *Healy* (1990)[71] adopted the 'absolute protection test' for evidence obtained by reason of breach of a detained person's constitutional right of access to a lawyer. As between two alternate rules or principles governing the exclusion of evidence obtained as a result of the invasion of personal rights of citizens, the court has, according to Finlay, an obligation to choose the principle which is likely to provide stronger and more effective defence and vindication of that right. That leads to the absolute protection rule of exclusion which he acknowledges places a limitation on the capacity of courts to arrive at truth and so administer justice. Chief Justice Finlay and the Supreme Court's 'bottom line' is as follows:

> The detection of crime and the conviction of the guilty no matter how important they may be in relation to the ordering of society cannot in my view outweigh the unambiguously expressed constitutional obligation 'as far as practicable to defend and vindicate the personal rights of the citizen.'

Does that sound even remotely like the language tenor or philosophy of recent legislative mores and political statements? What would then be the result of a clash, a conflict of principles? Judge Costello in *O'Leary* did allow the Oireachtas to depart from fundamentals like 'presumption of innocence' – on occasion – yet even then in accordance with 'principles' which he did not feel incumbent upon him (having found no violation) to enumerate. Certainly the courts can accommodate legislative change, as Judge Costello did. Interpretation is a creative function (of statutes and constitutions both). Yet quiescent in the instructions to the courts to implement changes in accordance with '*justice*' (e.g. in the 1992 Act), are either the seeds of the Acts own destruction, or the advent of an era of extreme judicial causistry, or both.

Within the legislative arena the all-out failure to pose those questions and their relegation to a separate arm of government is not only causistic but dishonest. A democratic process is characterized by the openness of the debate, not simply the tenor of the debate. Indeed there is something vaguely chilling about reading the Dáil Reports on these pieces of legislation. The almost overwhelming consensus across party lines that these changes are a 'good' thing and to be welcomed, particularly in the context of admittedly 'guillotined' and 'firebrigade' procedures is staggering.[72] It is only matched in stupefication by the overwhelming identification of politicians with victims of crime (particularly muggings, burglaries). What of the imaginative equation of being on the other side? How would that affect these assumptions?

DEBATING FUNDAMENTAL PRINCIPLES

Others, who have perhaps made that intuitive leap have suggested candidates for current, or possible, principles in criminal law. Zuckerman, for example, suggests that there are two fundamental principles of morality in this area of the law: the presumption of innocence, and proof beyond reasonable doubt.[73] He claims that all the stuff of procedure and rules of evidence can and should be explicable in terms of that dualism. Perhaps he is right – certainly they are constitutionally mandated in our jurisdiction. They may well form the basis of our ostensible bias. Interestingly, the judiciary in Ireland has given many of the rules of evidence and procedure a constitutional home, on the basis that they are 'fundamental' or 'core' or 'fair' procedure. Ashworth's candidates are threefold: the principle of mens rea (criminal intent), the principle against constructive liability, and the presumption of innocence.[74] Potential candidates for the reasons for departure from same would be: seriousness of offence; offence of a specific nature; speed and efficiency. Certainly, recent changes in the Irish context would seem to be reflective of that kind of assessment, yet nowhere is it acknowledged that this is happening. Instead legislation (change) is introduced as a panacea for public outcry.

In the US the Rodney King case – called a 'political prosecution' by defense lawyers – arguably served the same purpose, ostensibly leaving untouched the keystones or nature of the process thereby guaranteeing perhaps the quality of the verdict.[75] The trial or process in terms of going through the motions is still important. Our collective conscience remembers that is how we introduced justice, through the medium of procedure, but how those motions are gone through is not as important as the result. 'We want justice' were the words of LA Congress woman Maxine Waters prior to the second King trial.[76] It is axiomatic that justice should not only be done but be seen to be done, yet when viewed closely or in context, the *appearance* may now be what is overwhelmingly important. The Rodney King trial in LA, like the 'Supergrass' trials in Northern Ireland, begin to look, through this lense, much like show trials.[77]

Another instance of procedure or process and its mutation is found in the context of the recent Beef Tribunal enquiring into the sales of beef from Ireland into EC Intervention.[78] It is a tribunal of inquiry – not a court – though headed by the President of the High Court with the power to call witnesses. (It is 'white-collar crime' at its best; staffed by the ablest of Irish lawyers while the lowest District Court level of the criminal process is stuffed with indigent, frequently unrepresented defendants.) A challenge was made to Tribunal procedures by Goodman's lawyers which went to the Supreme Court. It was contended that the proceedings were unconstitutional, in not according due process or fair procedure to Goodman by adhering to all of the rules of evidence in its proceedings. The challenge was ultimately unsuccessful but the Supreme Court acknowledged that the constitutional right to fair procedure did require adherence to many of the rules of evidence and incorporated notions like cross-examination, the right to confront etc. Interestingly one of the Supreme Court judges also took the opportunity to address the suitability of the *process* here (a tribunal hearing) quite apart from its adherence to procedure. His comments are worth quoting in full:

> The trial and finding of guilt of political opponents and dissenters in such a way is a valuable instrument in the hands of governments who have little regard for human rights. Experience in many countries shows that persons may be effectively destroyed by this process. The fact that punishment by fine or imprisonment does not automatically follow may be of no importance; indeed a government can demonstrate its magnaminity by not proceeding to prosecute in the ordinary way. If a government chooses not to prosecute the fact that the finding is not binding on any court is of little comfort to the person found guilty; there is no legal proceeding which he can institute to establish his innocence. If he is prosecuted, the investigations and findings may have created ineradicable prejudice. This latter possibility is too abstract or remote from the case. We were informed that the public conduct of these proceedings was intended to have a 'cleansing effect'.[79]

The context, of course, is that of 'white collar' crime. Nonetheless it is evident from this, and the other judicial statements from the bench, that the concept of process, fair procedure and its constituent elements, under our system of legal adjudication is one meeting with a fair measure of judicial support and elucidation.

Those comments are of course made in the locus of the criminal justice system and in particular of the trial. Focusing on them suffers from the academic myopia of appealitis (assuming the trial to be paradigmatic or central) when the reality of the true pragmatic impact of the criminal justice system on citizens lives has been found to have moved correspondingly backward in time, with its encrustration of procedure: from trial to pre-trial, interrogation room to police car, video-tape to pre-video conversations. In a tragic sense the Rodney King case has all elements; the immediacy of policing on the street which only by happenstance came into the court. The trial has had in the US and elsewhere a focus and a visibility – it forces us perhaps to ask questions and anguish over values – or it should. Yet why has this has occurred more in the US than here?

Perhaps because (as American audiences would say) our government can so readily and speedily assuage public disquiet with legislative response. The American process is not as vulnerable or facilitative to quick legislating. Perhaps also that society (unlike ours) has not got the security of having an (unnecessary) emergency regime to guarantee (conceal) the state's benevolence, so it looks to its laurels – the actual system – to define it by examination, not contrast. I would argue that the problem in Ireland (and in the UK) has been the focus of concentration on the shadowy areas of our justice system, to define our 'lights'. It may be a dangerous assumption to assure ourselves of their existence because it is darker over there. It may be that we are looking in the wrong direction, or are having our attention deflected, or worse still, not looking at all.

6. QUESTIONS

WHAT IS THE ROLE AND VALUE OF PROCEDURE IN LATE TWENTIETH-CENTURY IRELAND?

Traditionally, and currently, it has been the maintenance of balance between citizen and state, a bias towards the individual accused, a definite political preference. Can we not now change that if we wish? Certainly the equation or formula used by our legislators inserts the victim into that balance, and adjusts the scales accordingly. What is the significance of that for the experience of those caught within that process – the accused?

The guaranteeing of individual rights in the 'traditional' manner has been deemed valuable by the state, believed worthy by the citizens, yet mitigated by the manner and context of its vindication; the reality of its value being dependant on the vagaries of the judiciary, the invocation of the criminal process (trial) and the resultant repercussions for certain classes who disproportionately represent both sides of the scale – victims and accuseds. Is there then a value here worth fighting for? Does the granting of individual rights serve a particular (political) purpose – a 'corporatist' one perhaps – keeping us individually aware, alert and 'guaranteed' of our rights, while politically (collectively) dormant or unaware of our position?

Michael Mandel makes that very point in the context of s. 24 of the Canadian Charter of Rights and Freedoms which encapsulates the exclusionary rule.[80] It is not aimed, he says, at controlling police misbehaviour, but rather at protecting the *system* from disrepute. It therefore fulfills a 'PR' function. Interestingly, the American and Canadian tendency is for the exclusionary rule to have greatest effect in less serious cases. The disrepute after all is greater if it is a serious offence and one acquits the accused.[81]

Mandel also suggests that there is a crisis of confidence in the criminal justice system's failure to deliver the goods. So one has an emphasis on underlying social values. In other words it is not the certainty of the conviction that matters, as much as its quality. In the eighteenth century formalism gave the 'bloody and repressive' regime a legitimacy.[82] Attention to form then becomes the hallmark of a legitimate system of justice. Therein lies the nexus of the English 'show trial'. Mandel suggests a deeper logic behind this: 'Substituting the abstract for the concrete in an attempt to make the divided appear united is a tactic central to legalised politics.' Looked at in this fashion the lawyers (judges) begin to look more like rulers – unrestrained – as the Charters/Constitutions are 'mostly a collection of vague incantations of lofty but entirely abstract ideals incapable of either restraining or guiding the judges in their application to everyday life'.[83]

We are closer to the rule of lawyers than the rule of law. Michael Zander who is a proponent of the value of having a Charter or Constitution in a jurisdiction, as a focus for the debate on principles or rights makes the point that it is important to get the balance right; that it is plainly unsatisfactory if it is wrong, and that courts are as sensible and competent as legislators.[84]

Certainly it is hard to argue with that in the Irish context. The legislators' recent attempt to reform the law in the context of the Criminal Evidence Act 1992 and the Criminal Justice Act 1993 has produced a hotchpotch of changes in legal rules which do not emanate from any particular perspective as to values or inherent principles of political morality in that system.

It is interesting to look at the origins of these changes. Their conception is acknowledged by politicians to have followed a route from the Law Reform Commission (itself initiated politically) Consultation Paper and Report process, to law. It is this sequence that has characterized the genesis of that group of legislation comprising the Criminal Law (Rape) Amendment Act 1990, the

Criminal Evidence Act 1992 and the Criminal Justice Act 1993. By definition, the inquiries engaged in by the Law Reform Commission are limited in scope, and from the inception, they are specific to certain issues which may tend to be 'political' hot-potatoes. So it is that we have Commission reports on sexual abuse of children, rape and so on. The government receive the imprimatur of 'dealing' with these issues, by referring them to the Commission. The Commission engages in an inquiry as to the legal position here and in other jurisdictions – a commendable and perfectly 'respectable' task – but in terms of the 'reform' as opposed to the 'law' part, necessarily treads into the territory of 'political' choice. How is the Commission informed? Does it have a direct line into the bloodstream of the Irish people? That task is the responsibility of politicians. Yet quite often on these issues the practice of seeking a 'legal' solution removes their political accountability. So it is that the Commission (made up of lawyers and laypersons) engages in debate. (This is a relatively recent development of the Commission.) They produce a consultation paper, invite written submissions and produce a report for the Government. The Commission may hold a 'seminar' at which interested groups or persons work as a 'think-tank' and a debate takes place.

This process has produced much heated debate, and recently a clash of culture between those orientated towards a 'medical' (victim centred) culture and those of a legal disposition (focused on the accused for example). The result may not be entirely satisfactory to either side. In terms of debate of the initial paper's positions, the Commission has been influenced however. The volte-face in their rape report of 1988 where they departed from the Consultation Paper's (1987) endorsement of a narrowly defined 'traditional' view of rape is an example of this influence. Having heard submissions from various groups, the report endorsed a broader gender neutral view. Interestingly on that occasion the minister went back to the paper's view for his initial bill, though at a later stage Minister

Ray Burke introduced a 'fourth' component offence: 'Rape under s. 4' to address concerns communicated to him in particular, by women's groups.

This example illustrates the way in which the debate (if any) is conducted, not through the political process (initially) but *legally*; politicians classify an emergency issue as legal and so sideline it. It may eventually disappear as issues dissipate and the emergent Commission report may gather dust on the legislative shelf.

Alternatively, the process may operate to give the 'guise' of controlled consultation, within a format which does not mandate democratic accountability and controls the debate.

It can ultimately be adopted or ignored, but the 'micro' approach will have ensured that although marginally democratic, the debate and its resultant reforms will be piecemeal; there will be no questioning of the general principles or political choices raised, and the responsibility ultimately shirked by politicians.

Whether one adopts Mandel's line as to the superficial role of procedure, or Thompson's line regarding its worth, it is clear that both are correct in the Irish context in so far as the legal process is utilized for resolution of political hot potatoes: not just substantively, which is a familiar process, but procedurally. A similar theme informs the demand for justice (i.e. a guilty verdict) in the King case, as is found in the Irish legislature's response to recent 'crises' by their legal resolution. The loser in terms of *process* may be the citizen accused.

IS THERE AT THE HEART OF THE IRISH CRIMINAL JUSTICE SYSTEM A CRISIS OF POLITICAL MORALITY AND IF SO, IS THAT CRISIS INEVITABLE?

To the extent that we aspire to live in a democratic regime, which logically through the medium of its democratic process can reach any manner of decision, a conflict arises in the criminal justice system where we place limitations on democratic rule (or majority tyranny) by the specification of certain rights as fundamental.

The guardianship of these rights by a non-democratic institution (the Supreme Court) in Ireland (as in America) falls easy prey to the arguments of critics that there cannot be such values outside the writ of democratic provenance, or that if a society wishes to make such judgements the judiciary is not an appropriate or even effective mechanism for their vindication. On a very basic level the extent to which both jurisdictions engage in the process of judge-watching illustrates the extent to which the judiciary reflect the political tenor of the day.[85]

In a recent book entitled *Democracy and its Critics* (1989) Robert Dahl,[86] an American political theorist, states that the 'hardest case' to reject in the context of certain 'fundamental interests' having priority over the democratic process, is that arguing for vindication of the right to a fair trial in criminal cases. Dahl's thesis is of interest as his focus is on democracy as a *process* (rather than on a democratic process of collective decision making which produces desirable results). One of the issues he addresses is the extent to which certain fundamental interests should have priority over the democratic process, and the processes or institutions which can best be counted on to protect these interests.

Dahl offers three alternatives besides that of the non-democratic Supreme Court. Of interest, in terms of the demonstrated fragility of the latter solution in the Irish context, is that of the 'evolution of public opinion'. Dahl's approach to the question of what a person's 'fundamental' interests are and how we can know them is:

> A person's interest or good is whatever that person would choose with fullest attainable understanding of the experiences resulting from that choice and its most relevant alternatives.[87]

The significance for the Irish legislator or member of the public here, is that they are forced to consider their position from the viewpoint of the accused:

> To say that it is in A's interest to have a fair trial in criminal cases is equivalent to saying that if A understood the consequences of having or not having a fair trial he would insist on a fair trial.[88]

Ultimately Dahl makes the point that we cannot point to a universal best solution to the protection of fundamental rights. He claims that, 'specific solutions need to be adapted to the historical conditions and experiences, political culture and concrete political institutions of a particular country'.[89] Rather more ominous, given the preceding discussion of the current state of Irish 'political culture' and the level or lack of debate, is his following comment:

> To the extent that a people is deprived of the opportunity to act autonomously and is governed by guardians, it is less likely to develop a sense of responsibility for its collective actions. To the extent that it is autonomous, then it may sometimes err and act unjustly. The democratic process is a gamble on the possibilities that a people, in acting autonomously, will learn how to act rightly.[90]

It is arguable that in the Irish context, the debate or lack of it on the implications of the changes in our criminal justice system is a product of a failure of Irish society to develop a sense of responsibility for its collective actions. The myopia of its legislators is matched only by the willingness of the Irish public audience (sic) to accept uncritically readily proffered solutions. It has been queried the extent to which this may be reflective of a reaction fashioned by and endemic to a media led culture, yet there is no doubt we exhibit little in the way of conscience and no evidence of a desire, not least an ability, to act autonomously. The long-term implications of that kind of political climate are ominous:

> When the democratic process can no longer be sustained in the face of a weak or hostile political culture, it strains credulity to believe that primary political rights will be prescribed for long by Court or any other institutions.[91]

Of course Dahl's solution may not be feasible in our culture. It may well be that in developing a political culture cognizant of fundamental rights, and ceding their monitoring to our courts by placing them in our Constitution, we have managed to satisfy ourselves of their continuance while forgoing any responsibility ourselves. That kind of abdication *or* lack of political responsibility may have altered the tenor of our society in a way that is now neither truly democratic nor cognizant of fundamental interests or rights.

WHAT IS THE TRUE NATURE OF OUR SYSTEM?

The quiet revolution in the Irish Courts in *Quilligan* (1987)[92] where the Supreme Court sanctioned the wider use of the extraordinary power of arrest under s. 30 of the Offences Against the State Act, 1939; and in the decision of Judge Costello in the High Court in *O'Leary* v *AG* (1991),[93] where he found constitutional the reverse onus provisions (placing the burden of proof on an accused charged with *inter alia* membership of a proscribed organisation) moves us closer to an inquisitorial model of justice than we might ever acknowledge. Why is it disquieting that these 'extraordinary' legislative provisions (non-jury trial, powers of detention after arrest) can be found valid constitutionally? Because it says something about the uncertain nature of our constitutional precepts, or the causistry of our judiciary, or the clarity of the distinction between what is extraordinary and what is not? Or because it brings about a serious and fundamental change in our value system (like the introduction of certain changes by means of legislation) which is the result of 'legal' and not political debate and involves lawyers and courts and judges (not people) as the protagonists? The facility for, and danger of, judicial accommodation of change, has previously been evidenced in emergency (war) type situations, and can evidently be replicated in other 'crisis' situations. Take for example the internment of Japanese-Americans and its constitutionality. The comment of Justice Jackson (dissenting) in *Koremotsu* v *US*[94] gives precise expression to the dilemma. Faced with the military necessity of detaining some 112,000 Japanese and Japanese-Americans in the US, the military, it was alleged, could not 'conform to conventional tests of constitutionality'. Justice Jackson, however, refused to decide the constitutionality of wartime military decisions stating that 'a judicial construction of the due process clause that will sustain this order is a far more subtle blow to liberty than the promulgation of the order itself.'

Although occasional decisions like *Kenny* guarantee the 'quality' of Irish justice, it is important to recall that in England and Ireland only a small percentage of those taken in under emergency detention provisions are ever actually processed through the system or charged.[95] In a manner which parallels the containment of terrorism in Europe within Northern Ireland (despite spasmodic movements from indigenous groups like ETA or transnational terrorists like Red Brigade or Action Directe) and 'terrorists' in the United Kingdom within Northern Ireland (through exclusion orders), the operation of the criminal justice system occurs within working class areas which pay an often invisible price as the matter does not proceed to the (public) trial. (Working-class people are twice more frequently victim and accused.) Interestingly, Ministers and Judges with increased crime-risk and increased security, lead increasingly isolated lives and do not know that price. Their comments in the context of Dáil Debates would have themselves associated with the *victims* of crimes of a property-type nature, yet the changes in the law are as yet unrelated to those kind of offences. The concept of 'victim' is itself seen in a certain way and was challenged recently at a safety for women conference by one contributor:

> My point is about the *'hidden victims of crime'* . . . They are innocent of criminal behaviour but guilty of belonging to the family of a perpetrator. Usually they are women – mothers, wives and girlfriends of offenders and their children. The stigma of being the house the guards call to – the shame felt for what their spouse or son did; the rejection and isolation sometimes imposed by neighbours or friends if the crime committed is widely publicised or widely denounced. The feeling that somehow they are guilty of something which no one will talk about. Add to this the shock and loss experienced by families of the perpetrator if he goes to prison either on remand or on sentence, and you have the ingredients for total disintegration of a family unit. Numerous pieces of research have identified phases in this process described by women who have virtually been bereaved by the loss of their partner to prison, feelings of shock, uncertainty, searching, confusion and guilt appear to be a part of the process. Add to this financial uncertainty, change of status, managing children alone, try to visit the incarcerated individual often over long distances and with no extra financial resources and one gets some feeling of what is involved. Do these women and children deserve to be punished and rejected by society and if not what as individuals and communities can we do to help them retain dignity and meaning in their lives?[96]

The concept of 'victim' is thus seen to be a product of a certain value judgement or political choice predicated on the notion of what constitutes a 'loss' and what is deviant. It is the result of a particular and partial view. It is in similar vein to the choice or view of the meaning of 'freedom of movement' within the European Community; one which facilitates exception for Northern Irish 'terrorists', and most recently for Irish women.[97] The questioning of the centrality of the 'trial' process, the changes in procedure *within* the 'accusatorial' system bringing it closer to its European opposite, illustrate in similar fashion that distance between labels and reality; words and their meaning.

7. CONCLUSION

> If humankind cannot hear too much reality, then it can
> hardly be surprising if nations also hide from the truth:
> a life spent pretending perfection is far more pleasurable
> than one dogged by actual confrontation with actuality.[98]

If Gearty presents us with a fair assessment of the recent 'chassis' in the Irish criminal justice system, and of the reflections elsewhere – in LA and Europe – perhaps we can begin to address or 'name' the dilemmas within our system, and in that way give to our current illusions the reality of 'a common habitat and a Name': something that may at least give us, and give our criminal justice system, some reason.

In Sophocles' play Antigone's account of why she broke the law of the land [99] contains a concept of 'fundamentals' superceding the politics of the current realm. That concept is found reflected in the Irish judiciary's commitment to a series of principles underlying the criminal justice system, comprising the constitutional guarantee of fair procedure. That latter it has been suggested, may clash with changes introduced to the Irish criminal process in the wake of recent social or political 'events'. That the two can coincide without heralding an obvious crisis is because in addition to being constrained within certain covers (particular or specific, as opposed to general changes being the order of the day), the judiciary through the medium of concepts like 'fairness' and 'interests of justice' can mitigate the invocation of change to some degree and so provide a bulwark against revolution. The cracks, in other words, are papered over.

'Public opinion' has been central to the changes that have been wrought. Spurred on by perceived crises or events in the media, Irish legislators have rushed to assuage fears and temper particular concerns by changing laws to accommodate 'different' views. No one elucidates how those views are different or what they are different from, yet omnipresent seems to be the assumption that a structure remains *there*. It is the thesis of this pamphlet, however, that lurching from one media-inspired crisis to the next has not forstalled, and has indeed engendered, a much greater crisis or event. To date we have been correspondingly horrified and reassured by the stories and their response. Just as 'law and order' campaigns need a constant and steady diet of crime, so 'victim-orientated' changes need a steady stream of such 'victims'. They have not been found wanting in Irish legislative life.

Yet as we sit in our private worlds watching tales of that public realm of crime being relayed in a sequence of fear, loathing and retribution, the kind of catharsis we feel is not analogous to that Grecian reflection on 'the other side'. Our response is not at all reflective or contemplative, but reactive. It is wedded in 'media' format to the '*moment*': what crime means *now*; what a victim feels *now*; what an accused merits *now*. Indeed even the recent change in the law admitting 'victim impact statements' on consideration of sentence, attempts to introduce a temporal 'freeze' on the victim's damage. Very many victim support workers feel these statements should go in only when the victim is still suffering damage from the crime: their 'value' being less if the victim has recovered.

It is this tension between the immediacy of response, the long history of our criminal justice structure, and the construction of a public opinion and set of values by reference to reportage today, which creates the climate of opinion of tomorrow, that foreshadows revolution. Derrida describes the implications thus:

> Think of the *immediately* international effects of the television of tomorrow on a public opinion that was first considered to be national. Think of the transformations that an opinion poll technique introduces where it can literally accompany, and even better produce the televised event – like the press this technique can surely give a voice to minorities deprived of institutional representation; it can correct errors and injustices; but this 'democratization' never legitimately represents. It never represents without filtering or screening – let us repeat it – a 'public opinion'. The 'freedom of the press' is democracy's most precious good, but to the degree that one has not at least granted rights, effectively in laws and in customs, to the questions that we have just been asking, this fundamental 'freedom' remains to be invented *every day*. At least. And democracy with it.[100]

An appreciation of the larger politics of what is happening requires us to look behind labels and words: to see if we are not so much comfortable with their meaning, as comfortable with their *actual* meaning. Looking at what is being done today, in the name of yesterdays norms may lead us to re-examine our beliefs and state what they are. Not to have clear policy objectives in the criminal justice system from prosecution to parole, is to risk more than confusion – it risks liberty. There had been a balance struck between individual and state. It evolved over time and through the medium of encrusting the criminal process with procedure. We may now have begun to dismantle it. Of course that process had its roots in an earlier, more repressive regime, yet it remained, as even rulers ceded to its manner of adjudication. It became a bulwark *on occasion* against state power, and that occasion gave it credence. Thompson sees that process as a virtue and cautions against its abandonment: '. . . watch this new power for a century or two before you cut your hedges down'.

Although dangers may manifest themselves in the form of new or disparate offences it is more odious to contemplate the loss of the process in the use of these offences against a citizen:

> . . . there is a difference between arbitrary power and the rule of law. We ought to expose the shams and inequities which may be concealed beneath this law. But the rule of law itself, the imposing of effective inhibitions upon power and the defence of the citizen from power's all-intrusive claims, seems to me an unqualified human good. To deny or belittle this good is, in this dangerous century when the resources and pretension of power continue to enlarge, a desperate error of intellectual abstraction. More than this, it is a self-fulfilling error, which encourages us to give up the struggle against bad laws and class-bound procedures and to disarm ourselves before power. It is to throw away a whole inheritance of struggle about *law*, and within the force of law, whose continuity can never be fractured without bringing men and women into immediate danger.[101]

Precisely because we are ceding ground on that process in this jurisdiction, the threat from an ever-expanding criminal calender becomes greater. The creation of categories of offences which will criminalize the activities of certain classes in Irish society (see above

Criminal Justice (Public Order) Bill 1993) is but the second stage of a happening. The first — securing their effective and efficient use — is the more vital to the State.

Action as a political priority has certainly inspired a rash of recent legislation. Yet it is the precise failure to put that action or its repercussions in a context, that is criticized. In England, by contrast, a comprehensive review of the criminal process was carried out in the wake of concern regarding miscarriages of justice and abuse of police powers.[102] While there was and will be dissent with regard to some of its proposals, there is the beginning of dialogue, because such a document inevitably touches on the *general principles* which inform a system *before* addressing *particular concerns*. Certainly principles will and do change: a mature society cannot only handle but welcome that development. It is change without principled reflection that indicates at best confusion, or careless inadvertence, at worst vested interests, ideological bankruptcy or dishonesty.

NOTES

1. *The Irish Times*, 3 July, 1993

2. Thomas S. Kuhn, *The Structure of Scientific Revolution*, (Second Edition), University of Chicago, 1970, p. 92.

3. The 'Gibraltar incident' refers to the shooting dead of three unarmed suspected terrorists on Gibraltar, by a special division of the British army who were following them (1988). The incident is now 'virtually certain' to be the subject of a full hearing of the European Court of Human Rights (*Irish Times*, 7 Sept., 1993). LA refers to the video taped beating of an African-American, Rodney King, by four white officers of the Los Angeles Police Department, following a traffic violation.

4. William O. Douglas, *Being an American*, John Day, New York 1948.

5. Witness the recent changes under the Criminal Law (Sexual Offences) Act 1993, relating to the decriminalization of male homosexual acts.

6. Roberts A. Dahl, *Democracy and its Critics*, Yale University Press, New Haven and London, 1989, p. 64.

7. Colin Summer, 'Rethinking deviance: towards a sociology of censure' in Colin Summer (ed.), *Censure Politics and Criminal Justice*, Open University Press, Milton-Keynes, 1990, p. 27.

8. Colin Summer, 'Reflections on a sociological theory of criminal justice systems', ibid., p. 42.

9. Law Reform Commission of Canada Report, *Our Criminal Law*, Ottowa, Canada, 1976.

10. Milan Kundera, *The Unbearable Lightness of Being*, Faber and Faber, London, 1948.

11. Bunreacht na h-Éireann (Constitution of Ireland). Enacted by the people, 1 July 1937.

12. Section 30 of the Offences Against the State Act, 1939, provides for an initial period of detention following an arrest (in relation to a 'scheduled' offence) of twenty-four hours, with a further possible period of twenty-four hours being sanctioned.

13. Hay, Linebough, Rule, Thompson, Winslow (eds.), *Albion's Fatal Tree: Crime and Society in Eighteenth-Century England*, Partheon, New York, 1975. E.P. Thompson, *Whigs and Hunters: The Origin of the Black Act*, Penguin, London,1990.

14. Both the Single European Act and the Maastricht Treaty supercede our Constitution, and indeed like our initial membership of the European communities, required Constitutional amendments and referenda.

15. Concern that ultimately proved to be unwarranted given the Supreme Court decision in *DPP* v *Quilligan* (1987) ILRM 600, which sanctioned the use of section 30 in relation to 'non-subversive' crime.

16. The Criminal Justice Act 1984 provides for an initial period of six hours detention, with a possible further six hour period. Since the clock stops running between midnight and 8 a.m. a total potential period of detention of twenty hours is provided for.

17. The first Prevention of Terrorism Act was enacted in 1974 and was confined to terrorism relating to Northern Ireland. It banned the Irish Republican Army, and provided for the 'exclusion' of persons from Great Britain or the United Kingdom, and permitted the police to hold persons for questioning for up to seven days at ports or airports and for up to forty-eight hours elsewhere, with the Secretary of State's approval, which latter detention could be extended for up to a further five days. Since 1984 the Act has been extended to cover international as well as Irish terrorism. 'Exclusion orders' however, can only operate in respect of persons, whom to the Secretary of State's satisfaction are involved in Northern Ireland related acts of terrorism. Lord Colville in his 1986 and 1987 reviews of the Act recommended the power to issue them altogether should be removed. Despite considerable pressure, however, the government retained this exceptional power to deal with an exceptional problem

during the parliamentary debate on part II of the 1989 bill. It is also noteworthy that proscription is an anti-terrorist tactic deemed useful only in relation to Northern Irish terrorism.

18. The Lavinia Kerwick incident arose out of her dissatisfaction with a suspended sentence handed down to William Conry (her former boyfriend), on 15 July 1992 on his pleading guilty to having raped her. Lavinia Kerwick became the first Irish rape victim to go public on the issue, thereby waiving her anonymity. The ensuing public debate centered on matters related to the trial and sentencing of sexual offenders generally. (See further: Kate Shanahan, *Crimes Worse than Death*, Attic Press, Dublin, 1992.

19. Stephen Vincent Benet, *John Brown's Body* (traditional).

20. Paul Auster, 'The Locked Room' in *The New York Trilogy*, Faber and Faber London, Boston, 1985, 1987, p. 221.

21. Douglas Hay 'Property, Authority and the Criminal Law' in *Albions Fatal Tree: Crime and Society in Eighteenth-Century England*, op. cit.

22. E. P. Thompson, *Whigs and Hunters: The Origin of the Black Act*, op. cit., p. 268.

23. William Twining, *Rethinking Evidence: Exploratory Essays*, Basil Blackwell, Oxford, 1990, p. 10.

24. Jack B. Weinstein, 'Considering Jury 'nullification': when may and should a jury reject the law to do justice', *American Criminal Law Review*, vol. 30, 239.

25. In the past they were mostly male property owners until *de Burca* v *Attorney General* (1976), IR38. De Burca successfully challenged the constitutionality of that provision which automatically excluded women from jury service.

26. *Report of the Government Advisory Committee on Fraud*, Stationery Office, Dublin, December 1992.

27. Royal Commission on Criminal Justice – established in March 1991 following the release of the Birmingham Six after seventeen years in

prison. Reported 6 July, 1993. (*Guardian*, 7 July, 1993. *The Times*, 7 July, 1993)

28. Rodney King was the victim of police assault on being stopped by the Los Angeles Highway Patrol for speeding on the night of 3 March, 1991. An amateur video of the incident, showing officers of the LAPD beating King, led to the trial of four officers in relation to the incident. They were incidentally acquitted of charges of assault by a jury drawn from a community outside Los Angeles, where the trial was held, known to contain a high percentage of retired police officers. That jury was predominantly white. The officers are white. King is black. Following that acquittal, the city of Los Angeles experienced a wave of violence, now known as the LA Riots. These were concentrated in the largely black, economically deprived city centre areas like South Central LA.

    The four officers were then charged with the federal charge of violating King's civil rights. The location of the second trial was South Central LA, with a more racially representative jury. Defense lawyers called it a 'political prosecution' (*see* 'Roll the Tape Again', *Newsweek*, 8 February, 1993.

29. These comments follow on an observation of the 'voir-dire' procedure comprising video instructions and selection of criminal trial jury in Pensacola, Florida, (Circuit Judge Green presiding). The opportunity was made possible through the Mary Ball Washington Foundation and the good offices of Circuit Judge Nancy Gillam.

30. *New York Times*, 7 February, 1993 E.7.

31. Morgantaler was a Canadian physician who was charged several times with contravening the Canadian Criminal Code by setting up free-standing abortion clinics. Even in the predominantly Catholic province of Quebec he was acquitted by jury trial.

    Clive Ponting ('whistle-blower') was a civil servant who leaked confidential documents to a labour MP concerning the sinking of the General Belgrano in the Falklands War. He was acquitted by jury trial.

32. E.P. Thompson, *Whigs and Hunters: The Origin of the Black Act*, op. cit., fn. 22, pp. 188–9

33. This Committee was established in June 1992 by the then Minister for Justice Padraig Flynn ' . . . to cover all aspects of the legal, technical and organisational aspects of the criminal justice response to serious fraud'.

34. ibid., para 8.3, p.56

35. ibid., para 8.7, p.56

36. The Criminal Evidence Act 1992, Part II makes provision for the admissibility of 'business records' in criminal trials.

37. Part III of the Criminal Evidence Act 1992 makes particular provision for the giving of testimony by certain witnesses (video, live TV link etc. see below).

38. The context was that of the second stage (Seanad, 24 March 1993, p. 28) of the Criminal Justice Bill 1993, a forerunner of the current Public Order Bill, introduced by the Progressive Democrats as a private members bill.

39. *McNabb* v *US*, (1943) 318 US 324, 347. J. Frankfurter: 'the history of liberty, has largely been the history of procedural safeguards'.

40. Packer, *The Limits of the Criminal Sanction*, Stanford University Press, 1968. Packer presents two models of the criminal justice system: 'due process' and 'crime control'.

41. *Miranda* v *Arizona* (1966) 384 US 436.

42. *The People (AG)* v *O'Brien* (1965) IR 142.

43. Section 78(1) of the Police and Criminal Evidence Act of 1984: 'In any proceeding the court may refuse to allow evidence in which the prosecution proposes to rely on to be given if it appears to the court that, having regard to all the circumstances, including the circumstances in which the evidence was obtained, the admission of the evidence would have such an adverse effect on the fairness of the proceedings that the court ought not to admit it.'

44. Section 24(2), Canadian Charter of Rights and Freedoms (1982).

45. Criminal Law (Rape) (Amendment) Act 1990 makes provision that rape and sexual assault cases be heard 'in camera' i.e. behind closed doors.

46. Criminal Justice Bill, 1992. Presented by the Minister for Justice, 30 Sept. 1992. Long Title: An Act to Enable the Court of Criminal Appeal to Review Unduly Lenient Sentences, to Make Other Provisions in Relation to Sentencing, to Provide for the Payment by Offenders of Compensation for Injury or Loss Resulting from their Offenses and to Provide for Corrected Matters. This was the fore-runner of what is now the Criminal Justice Act 1993.

47. Criminal Evidence Act 1992. Long title: An Act to Amend the Law of Evidence in Relation to Criminal Proceedings and to Provide for Connected Matters.

48. The references are to some Irish instances of 'miscarriages of justice'. (For some reason the cases seem to have followed numerically: Birmingham Six, Guilford Four, Winchester Three . . .) The 'Tallaght Two' case refers to the conviction of two young men from Tallaght, Dublin in relation to the theft of a motor-vehicle. The evidence against them was primarily that of visual identification by the owner, who clung to the hood as they escaped. It later emerged as a result of a TV investigation that forensic evidence (of a fingerprint) which would have substantiated the boys' account, was not revealed by the prosecution.

   Nicky Kelly's conviction in relation to the infamous Sallins mail-train robbery, was on the basis of a confession obtained under interrogation. Kelly fled the jurisdiction, his fellow accused were successful in appealing their convictions, yet Kelly on his return was imprisoned, later released and granted a full pardon. However his attempt to challenge the conviction by route of a later civil action was 'estopped' as being an 'abuse of the process of the court' (*Kelly* v *Ireland* (1986), ILRM 318).

   The *Lynch case* (*DPP* v *Lynch* (1982) IR 64) is perhaps the least well known, but once again a conviction was based on a confession obtained under interrogation (of twenty-two hours duration) and later revealed in the Supreme Court, to be contrary to factual evidence, substantiating Lynch's denial of the murder charge.

All these cases illustrate the fragility, vulnerability and inaccuracy of the Irish criminal justice system. They also reveal its limited facility for dealing with miscarriages of justice. The latter lacunae was addressed by the Martin Commission in its Report, yet its recommendation of a 'review tribunal' has not yet borne fruit. (Martin Committee Report: *Report of the Committee to Enquire into Certain Aspects of Criminal Procedure*, 1990. Chairman Judge Frank Martin)

49. This second federal trial resulted in the conviction of two of the four officers. The verdict was in large measure accepted by those in the community of South Central Los Angeles, who had been critical of the verdict of the first trial.

50. Contrast with the 'finality' given verdict in the *Herrera* case by the US Supreme Court, where the facility for appeal in 'miscarriage of justice' cases was greatly reduced. *Herrera* v *Collins*, US Supreme Court, 25 Jan. 1993 (*New York Times*, 26 Jan. 1993).

51. Rush Limbaugh hosts both a radio and TV 'talk show' carried on the major networks and broadcast throughout the US. He has recently used these shows to display his ongoing distaste for the newly incumbent Clinton administration. He is one of many (powerful and mostly conservative) voices in the American media. (*See* 'The Power of Talk: How Call-in Shows are Shaking up Politics', *Newsweek* 8 Feb., 1993).

52. Richard Sparks, *Television and the Drama of Crime: Morality and the Place of Crime in Public Life*, Open University Press, Buckingham, 1992, p. 155.

53. ibid.

54. *Antigone* in Sophocles' *The Three Theban Plays: Antigone, Oedipus the King, Oedipus at Colonus*, Penguin, London, 1984, pp. 67–8

55. ibid., pp. 81–82.

56. William Conry was the accused in the Lavinia Kerwick case who pleaded guilty to having raped her. The Kilkenny incest case refers to the plea of guilty entered by a father of a twenty-seven year-old woman from Kilkenny in relation to charges of perpetrating incest and assault upon her over a period of sixteen years. (*See The Kilkenny Incest Case as told to Kieron Wood*, Poolbeg, Dublin, 1993)

57. See generally Dáil and Seanad debates on the Criminal Evidence Act 1992 and the Criminal Justice Act 1993. (*Criminal Evidence Act 1992* – Dáil: 18 Feb '92, 3 March '92, 5 March '92, 6 March '92; Committee: 8 April '92, 26 May '92, 27 May '92; Report and final stages: 24 June '92; Seanad: 1 July '92; *Criminal Justice Act 1993* – Dáil: 10 March '93, 11 March '93; Seanad: 24 March '93, 25 March '93)

58. Criminal Evidence Act 1992. Part II deals with documentary evidence and the admissibility thereof. Part III deals with the giving of testimony by witnesses in certain proceedings and Part IV the competence and compelability of spouses and former spouses to give evidence. Section 8 deals with the criteria for admissibility of documentary evidence, 'fairness to the accused' being part of that assessment. Section 16 regarding the admissibility of video evidence at trial again invokes the criteria interests of justice and its component – fairness to the accused. Section 29 makes special provision for the giving of evidence by those outside the state.

59. *DPP* v *T*, unreported Court of Criminal Appeal, 27 July 1988.

60. *Murphy* v *Dublin Corporation* (1972), IR 215

61. *DPP* v *McGrail* unreported Court of Criminal Appeal, 18 Dec. 1989.

62. *DPP* v *O'Reilly*, Court of Criminal Appeal, 26 April, 1990.

63. *State (Healy)* v *Donoghue* (1976), IR 325, 348.

64. *DPP* v *Egan*, Supreme Court, 30 May, 1990.

65. *O'Leary* v *AG*, Judge Costello, 26 October 1990.

66. *Mapp* v *Gilhooley*, Supreme Court, 23 April 1991.

67. *DPP* v *Kehoe*, Court of Criminal Appeal, *ex tempore*, Judge O'Flaherty.

68. *Goodman International* v *Judge Hamilton, Ireland and the Attorney General*, unreported Supreme Court, 1 November 1991.

69. *DPP* v *Kenny* (1990), ILRM 569.

70. The suggestion that the recent English 'PACE' decisions excluding evidence have only related to confession cases and not to those where the existence of the evidence and its probity is undeniable and so more difficult to resist or refuse.

71. *DPP* v *Healy* (1990), ILRM 313.

72. Both the Criminal Evidence Act 1992 and the Criminal Justice Act 1993 were rushed through the Houses of the Oireachtas by means of the operation of a 'guillotine' to cut off debate. In the course of contributions on both bills the words 'emergency' and 'firebrigade' measures appear, together with copious references to the crises, particularly with regard to the 1993 Act, both Lavinia Kerwick and the Kilkenny incest case being invoked.

73. Zuckerman, *The Principles of Criminal Evidence*, Clarendon, Oxford, 1989.

74. A. Ashworth, 'Towards a Theory of Criminal Legislation', *Criminal Law Forum* 41, 1989.

75. Comment by a juror in first few minutes of jury retiring to consider its verdict in *Twelve Angry Men*, film directed by Sidney Lumet. USA United Artists MGM/UA Home Video (1990): 'He got a fair trial – what more do you want? God knows what it cost'.

76. Maxine Waters is an African-American congresswoman from Los Angeles. She made this remark on American television the morning of the 'second trial'.

77. In similar fashion to the movement from internment in Northern Ireland to the Diplock Court system was thought progressive. Lord Diplock was appointed to chair a committee to look into the practice

of internment without trial of suspected terrorists in Northern Ireland. The committee was set up on 22 September 1972 to consider 'what arrangements for the administration of justice in Northern Ireland could be made in order to deal more effectively with terrorist organization by bringing to book, otherwise than by internment by the Executive, individuals involved in terrorist activities, particularly those who plan and direct, but do not necessarily take part in, terrorist acts; and to make recommendations. (*Report of the Commission to consider legal procedures to deal with terrorist activities in Northern Ireland.* Chairman: Lord Diplock. Dec. 1972 CMND 5185.)

The result of the implementation of the Report was the 'non-jury' Diplock Court structure now operative in Northern Ireland. The criminal cases are heard by a judge sitting alone (the Irish Special Criminal Court has three judges) operating modified rules of evidence allowing for ready reception of confession evidence and very strict bail requirements.

78. In brief the allegation was that Goodman International engaged in questionable practices in the processing of beef in Ireland, thus defrauding both the Government and EC.

79. Judge Hederman, *Goodman International* v *Justice Hamilton Ireland and the Attorney General*, Supreme Court, 1 Nov. 1991 referring to the dissent of Judge Murphy in the High Court in Australia: *Victoria* v *Australian Building Construction Employees and Builder's Labourers Federation* (1981–1982, 152 CLR 26).

80. Michael Mandel, *The Charter of Rights and the Legalization of Politics in Canada*, Wall & Thompson, Toronto, 1989.

81. *US* v *Leon* (1983), 468 US 897 developed the 'good faith' exception to the exclusionary rule under American law.

82. E.P. Thompson, *Whigs and Hunters*, op. cit. and Hay, Rule, Thompson, Winslow (eds) *Albion's Fatal Tree*, op. cit.

83. Michael Mandel, *The Charter of Rights and the Legalization of Politics in Canada*, op. cit, fn. 80.

84. Michael Zander, *A Matter of Justice: The Legal System in Ferment*, Oxford University Press, Oxford, 1989.

85. Witness the concerns of Irish women's groups that there be a female judge appointed to a recent vacancy on the Irish Supreme Court, and the controversy in the United States regarding President Clinton's appointment to the vacancy secured by the retirement of Justice White (a conservative member).

86. Robert A. Dahl, *Democracy and its Critics*, Yale University Press, New Haven and London, 1989, p. 118

87. ibid. p. 180.

88. ibid: p. 181.

89. ibid. p. 192.

90. ibid. p. 193.

91. ibid. pp. 172, 173.

92. *DPP* v *Quilligan* (1987) ILRM 600.

93. *O'Leary* v *AG* (1991) ILRM 454.

94. *Koremotsu* v *US* (1944) 323 US.

95. From the beginning of 1984 to 31 March 1989, 889 people were arrested in Great Britain under the PTA in connection with Northern Irish terrorism: only 134 (15 percent) were later charged with criminal offences. (*See further*: Dicksen, Brice 'Prevention of Terrorism Act, 1989' NILQ 250, 1989, p. 256, fn. 29).

96. Ann Rynn, 'Working with perpetrators – what are the issues?', *Safety for Women Conference*, Dublin Castle, October 1992, p. 52.

97. This refers to the 'containment' of Irish women within Ireland as a result of the Supreme Court interpretation in *AG* v *X and others* (1992), ILRM 401, of the 'right to life of the unborn' provision in our Constitution (Article 40.3.3). This left the question of their right to travel in some doubt, one eventually resolved by Constitutional

amendment of Article 40.3.3 in December 1992 to the following effect: 'This subsection shall not limit freedom to travel between the state and another state'.

98. Conor Gearty, *Irish Times*, 4 Feb., 1993.

99. Sophocles, *Antigone*, op. cit. Part III.

100. Jacques Derrida, *The Other Heading: Reflections on Today's Europe*, Indiana University Press, Bloomington, 1992, pp. 97–98.

101. E.P. Thompson, *Whigs and Hunters*, op. cit. p. 266.

102. *Royal Commission on Criminal Justice.* Chairman: Viscount Runciman of Doxford CBE FBA, *Report* Presented to Parliament July 1993, Cm 2263 HMSO London.